THEO VON TAANE

P(
THE BE
NOTEBOOK
FOR POKÉMON GO FANS

Between author of this book and producers of Pokémon or one of its subsidiaries is no connection. This book is neither approved or supported by Nintendo nor of one of its subsidiaries and furthermore in any way connected with this parties.

Bibliografische Information der Deutschen Nationalbibliothek:
Die Deutsche Nationalbibliothek verzeichnet diese Publikation in der Deutschen Nationalbibliografie; detaillierte bibliografische
Daten sind im Internet über http://dnb.dnb.de abrufbar.
© 2017 Theo von Taane; 2. Auflage

Herstellung und Verlag: BoD – Books on Demand, Norderstedt

ISBN: 9783743160040

More books of Theo von Taane

book	ISBN / order nr.
FUNCRAFT - The unofficial Math Coloring Book: Minecraft Minis	9783743137523
FUNCRAFT - The unofficial Math Coloring Book: Superheroes in Minecraft Skin	9783743138025
FUNCRAFT - The best unofficial Math Coloring Book for Minecraft Fans	9783743138933
FUNCRAFT - The unofficial Notebook (quad paper) for Minecraft Fans	9783743148734
FUNCRAFT - The best unofficial Notebook (ruled paper) for Minecraft Fans	9783743154186
FUNCRAFT - Merry Christmas to all Minecraft Fans! (unofficial Notebook)	9783743149151
FUNCRAFT - Happy New Year to all Minecraft Fans! (unofficial Notebook)	9783743159976
Password Logbook for Minecraft Fans	9783743163386
Pokefun - The unofficial Notebook (Team Red) for Pokemon GO Fans	9783743159983
Pokefun - The unofficial Notebook (Team Yellow) for Pokemon GO Fans	9783743159990
Pokefun - The unofficial Notebook (Team Blue) for Pokemon GO Fans	9783743160002
Pokefun - The best unofficial Notebook for Pokemon GO Fans	9783743160040
Majestic Flowers and Butterflies - Adult Coloring Book	9783739227085
Football 2 in 1 Tacticboard and Training Workbook	9783734749605
Badminton 2 in 1 Tacticboard and Training Workbook	9783734749643
Baseball 2 in 1 Tacticboard and Training Workbook	9783734749650
Basketball 2 in 1 Tacticboard and Training Workbook	9783734749681
Bowling 2 in 1 Tacticboard and Training Workbook	9783734749698
Cricket 2 in 1 Tacticboard and Training Workbook	9783734749711
Ice Hockey 2 in 1 Tacticboard and Training Workbook	9783734749728
Fencing 2 in 1 Tacticboard and Training Workbook	9783734749735
Field Hockey 2 in 1 Tacticboard and Training Workbook	9783734749810
Football (Soccer) 2 in 1 Tacticboard and Training Workbook	9783734749827
Futsal 2 in 1 Tacticboard and Training Workbook	9783734749834
Handball 2 in 1 Tacticboard and Training Workbook	9783734749841
Lacrosse Women 2 in 1 Tacticboard and Training Workbook	9783734749858
Lacrosse Men 2 in 1 Tacticboard and Training Workbook	9783734749865
Netball 2 in 1 Tacticboard and Training Workbook	9783734749872
Rugby 2 in 1 Tacticboard and Training Workbook	9783734749889
Chess 2 in 1 Tacticboard and Training Workbook	9783734749896
Squash 2 in 1 Tacticboard and Training Workbook	9783734749902
Tennis 2 in 1 Tacticboard and Training Workbook	9783734749919
Table Tennis 2 in 1 Tacticboard and Training Workbook	9783734749926
Volleyball 2 in 1 Tacticboard and Training Workbook	9783734749933
Water Polo 2 in 1 Tacticboard and Training Workbook	9783734749940

...futher titles available and in preparation.

CPSIA information can be obtained
at www.ICGtesting.com
Printed in the USA
LVHW081026080622
720752LV00029B/872